The Butterfly Effect

Transform From Your Cocoon

DAROLYN MANGUM

ISBN-10:   0990989046
ISBN-13:   978-099098904-2
LCCN: 2013950826

Second Printing
Printed in the United States of America
10 9 8 7 6 5 4 3 2 1

Published by May House Press & Publications
Cover Illustration and Design by WOW Designs by Walt
Editing by Morissa Schwartz
Author photograph by Ke'Andra Beck Photography

DEDICATION

This book is dedicated to the fearless, independent, women who dared to let the world dictate who they became:

My hard-working & loving mother, Evelyn J. Tyler

My weekend TV buddy maternal grandmother, Hannah L. Johnson

My quiet spirited maternal great grandmother, Evelyn Robinson (Granny)

My Spiritual guide paternal grandmother, Geneva Tyler (Big Mama)

My wonderful mother-in-law, Leona Mangum

My "Teenage Porch Buddy," Gertrude Pierce

My "Real Life Mae West," Mary Provost

CONTENTS

ACKNOWLEDGMENTS

I am and will forever be indebted to many individuals who helped inspire me to make my dream of becoming an author a reality. There are people who knowingly and some unknowingly who contributed. It would take another chapter to thank everyone. This book was written from my personal experiences and experiences of others. Everything in the book may not be for everyone, but I can guarantee that everyone who reads it will relate to something that is said.

There are not enough words, pieces of paper, or time to thank my husband, Richard and my daughters Richelle and Richae' for their inspiration, love, patience, and encouragement. They all cheered me on every step of the way. Because of the three of them, I never felt alone on this journey. To my mother, Evelyn, for bringing me into this world and being a woman who always put everyone else before herself. My sisters, Sharon for your continuous prayers and spiritual guidance, Carlette and Kim for giving me life experiences to write about. ☺ My grandsons, Jayden and Landen, who inspired me by showing their excitement that I was actually writing a book; they were excited like I was famous. Just wait boys Mee Maw is working on that, it won't be long. ☺ MFA Carla for being a proofreader even though you don't read a lot. To Connie, for your prayers, loving support, and genuine tears of joy. To Marshall and Al, for their support and input from a male perspective. All of my former male co-worker buddies who had so many "interesting" stories they shared in my office. Who knew I would be writing a book and your stories would be an influence, I will never forget you all. ☺ To all of my friends, former co-workers, and family members who continued to encourage me. To my graphic designer and publisher, Shani and Walter for all of your patience. ☺ Thanks to Jay Barnett for creating the title for the book.

Last, but not least I thank God who in Jesus name gave me the wisdom, strength, courage, and guidance that allowed me to make it through this journey.

PART

1

The Cocoon Stage

A cocoon in the life cycle of the butterfly is known as a protective covering. In comparison to the cocoon stage of a butterfly, women are in the stage of learning, growing, and developing, so we are excused for many of the choices we make, this is a fragile stage of development. As cocoon's we need guidance, to be fed positive and motivational information, and need to be protected. There are many women who breeze through the cocoon stage, as they transform, bringing their dreams, desires, and ambitions into the caterpillar stage. While there are others who get stuck in the cocoon stage because they are afraid to step outside the box or they lack motivation, preventing their progress through their transformation. This stage is when our flight pattern is being mapped out; our self-esteem is influenced, and we can almost see ourselves coming out of our cocoon, but we are not sure we are ready. The cocoon is a comfort zone for many women; who are sheltered and protected from the elements of life. Women often tip out of their comfort zone, but realize they are not prepared to emerge, yet they realize they are outgrowing our covering. This can be compared to the caterpillar squirming to get out of the protective covering because there is not enough room to grow. A symbol of your cocoon can be moving out of your parent's home, being too dependent on a spouse, stuck in a career that you are not very excited about, stuck in an unhealthy relationship, or you are just afraid to make even small changes in your life because you are not sure of the outcome. Can you relate to feeling like it's time to emerge from your cocoon, but are afraid to do what it takes, because you don't have the confidence to leave the protection of your cocoon?

It's not who you are that holds you back, it's who you think you're not.

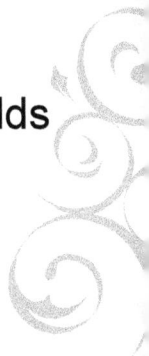

CHAPTER

1

"Pandora's Box"
There are Treasures in Your Life Waiting to be Explored.

As many of us know, fairy tales were told as a form of entertainment long ago. Families and friends would sit around and see who could tell the best stories. There were no televisions or radios to keep people entertained. Stories were passed down from generation to generation, parts were added and parts were taken away, which made the stories have different twists, beginnings, and endings. We are all familiar with The Three Bears, The Three Little Pigs, Snow White, and others to name a few. Although there are different versions for each tale, they end with the same message. However, many have heard, but do not know the tale of "Pandora's Box" which is told from a male's point of view.

The version of Pandora as I know was said to be the story of forbidden treasures and the curiosity of a woman. Pandora was a beautiful woman who was forbidden to open gifts given to her by the gods. Initially, the gifts were given to her in a jar, the jar became so full, the gifts were put into a treasure box. Pandora was told, if she opened the treasure box, she would cause misfortune and harm to mankind. The story of Pandora was told by Greek Mythology as an opportunity to discourage women not to be disobedient by limiting their curiosity regarding things they could achieve in life. If Pandora opened the box it was said that men would blame women for the evils of the world, a story similar to Adam and Eve. "Pandora's Box" became a tale that discouraged curiosity, encouraged obedience, which was a warning to women not to look within themselves or they would cause danger and destruction to themselves and others. The gifts inside the box were dazzling beauty, the ability to communicate through song and dance, creativity, guidance, independence, sensual desire, kindness, hope, love, honesty, and the largest gift was the gift of curiosity. Pandora suppressed the desire to look inside the box for a very long time. One day, Pandora could not resist the urge to look inside the box. This feeling can be related to women who have held back being who they want to be and doing what they want to do in order to fulfill roles and duties at home and work. They feel they want to evolve and explore life, but can't because of responsibilities. Pandora opened the box and immediately felt empowered to take possession of her gifts. Before she could embrace the excitement she felt, she was consumed with guilt, fear, discouragement, and unworthiness because she had been in the mindset that the gifts in the box were not for her they were for everyone else.

Does Pandora's story sound familiar to you? How often have women felt they could not follow their dreams because they do not realize the treasures within, or feel they do not have permission from others to explore their treasures? The story ends with Pandora being overwhelmed with emotions. She immediately tried to stuff the gifts back into the box. The feelings she felt were the feelings she was warned about. We have all had ideas, dreams, or aspirations that we held back because we did not have the support or encouragement to follow them. As she closed the box a quiet, still voice gave her permission to re-open it, the voice was the voice of Hope speaking to her to let her know that she could safely open the box and expose her treasures. What Pandora didn't realize was the treasures were already hers to begin with. Just like Pandora, there is a calm still voice that says, you can open the box and let your gifts flow free, but you have to give yourself permission to release your gifts and use them.

My Pandora experience is related to how I began exploring my treasures. I always believed that, "I can do all things through Christ who strengthens me." – Philippians 4:13.

I remember working as a school counselor, talking quite often about ideas and future goals to my co-worker, who was also a counselor. We would discuss our capabilities and the possibilities that life held for us. I felt in my heart that being a counselor was not the end of my career path, but I was not sure of what I wanted to do. There was so much I wanted to share with others, regarding life experiences. The bond my coworker and I had allowed me to stay grounded because there were days that I felt I was misplaced and hitting a dead end in my career. We had many opportunities throughout our years of working together, to laugh, talk and share feelings. If it wasn't for us having each other, I don't know how we would have made it. As a counselor you quickly realize that you also need someone to talk to and share your thoughts.

I remember telling my coworker one day, I was thinking of becoming a certified Life Coach. I felt confident in this decision and decided to research information on exactly what a Life Coach was. I contemplated that decision back and forth for two school years. Not that I didn't feel capable, but I was allowing myself like many women to become content in my career. After a while, I began to feel I was holding myself back from being the best I could be. Often times we know when we need to do something different, but those feelings of contentment comfort us enough to ignore moving forward. I began to pray and ask God for guidance and direction. The desire to be the best me I could be continued to get stronger and stronger, yet it wasn't strong enough for me to step outside of my box of contentment to pursue something new. I remember talking to my coworker about how I was feeling. I was a feeling overwhelmed and discouraged. We worked together as a team for five years before she was moved to another campus. The workload became unbearable, with me being the only counselor on the campus. Due to budget cuts, staff had to be reduced, which increased the workload of the existing staff. I began to pray and again ask for guidance, I was at a point where I was unhappy at work. My prayer was answered in an unexpected way. When we ask for God's assistance, expect the unexpected. I told a friend of mine, by the end of my contract for the 2013 school year; my career as a school counselor would be over. It was obvious things were not getting better. The majority of the staff in the district felt the feeling of dread and discomfort, some people were okay being miserable, I was not. They complained endlessly, every day. I felt I had to explore other options in order to make me happy to go to work. God was working out His plan for me all along.

An unfortunate situation arose that caused me to leave my employment nine months before my contract ended, which was before my projected date to pursue other options. Things happened so quickly, I did not have a plan, nor did I know what was ahead for me. Once I realized I could not emotionally or physically return to that job, the wheels in my mind started turning. This is when my Pandora box was opened. I began to realize everything happens for a reason. God said *my timing and His timing were not the same.* Initially, I questioned why this situation happened, I couldn't figure out the purpose besides the fact that my time was up in this position. After being off and having time to think, I realized that I had been given the opportunity to use my gifts and talents. My treasure box was full of untapped treasures, which were all tucked safely away until it was time for me to open it.

The feeling of knowing your gifts and talents are unlimited causes excitement beyond belief. Once your treasure box is opened the gifts pour out, you will be stunned as you sit back and watch the magic and beauty of God's work. My research into Life Coaching was not in vain. I got my certification, but did not stop there I began to explore other options and received my certification as an Anger Resolution Therapist. I realized there are endless career possibilities if you step outside of your comfort zone. I have always been a person that rarely met a stranger. As I looked back I had always been a "Life Coach," even as a teen. People always confided in me or came to me for advice. I remember for many years sitting countless hours on the phone or in person with family, friends, or co-workers listening and trying to help solve their problems. I realized helping others was one of my gifts. As I dug deeper into my treasure box I found I was also a leader. I never felt I was a follower, but I never looked at myself to be a leader. I felt I was just being me. I had someone say to me one day, "You have a great spirit, always have a kind word, and can turn any negative situation into a positive one. You are a great role model and can inspire everyone you meet. The world would be a better place if there were more people like you." The statement brought tears to my eyes and joy to my heart.

As I began to explore my career goals, I kept that statement in mind. God decided that it was time for me to help others that were not in my immediate circle. I woke up one morning and devised a business plan; ideas started flowing and were endless. I felt like a child at Christmas opening gifts and every gift was something they asked for. My prayers had been answered; God showered me with untapped gifts and talents to become a business owner. The gift that really surprised me, you are holding in your hands…the gift of becoming an author. Although I was certified as an English teacher, taught English from middle to high school, loved to read, I never considered writing a book. One night while in bed I was going over my business plan in my head, a still quiet voice whispered, "You should write a book, there are people that need to hear what you have to say, there are women who can be reached." I immediately thought...*me, write a book? About what, where do I start?* Of course, I could not go back to sleep because my mind was racing a thousand miles a minute, I was excited about the idea and decided I would do it. That day, I came up with several titles and began to write topics for chapters.

The treasures and gifts that have been unleashed within have amazed me. I had the key to my treasure box all along, but it took an unfortunate situation on my job, and lots of prayer to unlock my treasures. We all have to give ourselves permission to have confidence that we can do and be whatever we want to be. Pandora was not the only person blessed with treasures. Remember, "I can do all things through Christ who strengthens me." Philippians 4:13 applies to you, too.

Think About It!

What treasures are inside of your box waiting for permission to come out?

In order to see changes
in your life, you first have
to   make changes.

CHAPTER

2

It's Never Too Late
The Sky is the Limit

Unlike Visa, Master Card, or American Express, life has no limits when it comes to following your dreams. There are no written rules to say a person cannot go back to college, open a business, change careers, or start a hobby after a certain age or number of years. It is never too late to accomplish your dreams. We become our own limits when we talk ourselves out of taking steps we need in order to work towards our dreams. Naysayers can also convince us that our desires or passions can't be accomplished because we have "waited too long." As women, there are often obstacles that we have to overcome that can deter our dreams, but they do not have to be forgotten. Women need to give themselves permission to emerge and evolve in spite of obstacles. Every life has a season of change. Seasons of change come into a person's life when it's their turn. It could be a decision that weighs heavy on your heart regarding issues such as getting out of an unfulfilling relationship, going back to school, changing careers, starting your own business, or learning a new skill.

It is common for women to spend their 20's and 30's creating a home and building a family while trying to maintain balance and keep peace within. In order to keep peace and make things better for the family, women often compromise what they want simply to meet the needs of others. Women are wives, mothers, teachers, nurses, chauffeurs, and chefs before they ever leave home to go to the office for their "job." Working women have been heard saying at the end of their 8:00-5:00 job, "It's time for me to go to my *other* job." The old cliché, a women's work is never done, is not just a cliché but also a reality in the lives of many women. No matter what title women hold, they are often not the women they want to be. They settle into roles because that is the role they have to play during a particular season in their life. In society, a woman's primary role is to reproduce and be a nurturer; they are caring for everyone else's needs and often neglecting their own.

For a woman to take a new path and realize it's not too late to pursue her desires and become the woman she dreams of, she has to leave the old path and change her mind set. It doesn't mean neglecting her family or career obligations, but she must find time for herself. As mothers and wives, women get into the habit of considering everything and everyone else as a priority while failing to realize *she* is her priority. When a woman focuses solely on the needs of everyone else, she starts to neglect herself in ways that she does not realize until she is at her breaking point. Her body is exhausted from all of the duties she has and does not take the time to stop. Her mind is tired because it never turns off, even at rest, because she is always questioning whether or not she is doing all she can do and giving all she can give to everyone she is responsible for. Women must pay attention to their feelings, because feelings are reality and must be addressed.

Your body will tell you when it's time to take a break. Being unconscious of the emotional and physical needs of your body can take a toll on you after a period of time. The habit of ignoring the needs of your body disconnects you from emotions, which covers up unhappiness and pain. Many women are guilty of ignoring the needs of their bodies because they feel as though they have so much to do; she does not have time to worry about herself. The caretaker and "rescuer" role women play keeps them out of touch with their feelings.

What society considers a "good wife" or a "good mother" causes many women to lose themselves. How many women lose their identity because they are known for years as, Darrell's wife, Jayden's mother, or Landen's sister? The loss of identity is not done on purpose, it just happens because of the label society creates for certain roles. Identity is connected to the people you care for which is often a future setup for resentment and anger. As women get older and start to be less depended on by others, they often resent not having a life of their own outside of the roles they play. Many women feel that it is too late to be who they want to be because they have spent their lives nurturing and catering to others. Change can't and won't happen within until women allow themselves to be free of all that has been stuffed, stacked, denied, or ignored within them for years. Their emotional and physical energy needs to be recharged. Not every woman in the world has experienced the feelings described above. However, there are more women who can relate than women who cannot.

Learning to care for yourself and listen to your emotions is a process that many women have a hard time adjusting to. If more women would commit to changing their thoughts and living their lives fully, their circumstances will begin to change. This commitment is the first step to following their dreams. We must tune into our emotions to appreciate what our inner woman is telling us. There are women who feel the woman on the inside is waiting to get out, but rather than embrace the woman inside and allow her to emerge, they push her down and say, "Not yet." This talk between the inner woman and outer woman go on sometimes for years until one day the inner woman says, "I hope the world is ready, I am coming out!" At this point, there is no turning back because the suppressed woman has the strength and determination to pursue her dreams and nothing can hold her back.

I remember the feeling of kicking the cocoon skin off and becoming a caterpillar. My antennas were waving so that I could feel my way around the world. I didn't realize there was so much to be explored. I was very sheltered even as an adult. I didn't have to be, it was the only life I knew. I woke up one day and realized I had never experienced many things in life because I was so busy trying to be the best woman I knew how to be in my role as a wife and mother. I centered my life around my family. Everywhere I went, my daughters went. As they grew older and had their own lives, I realized that I didn't have a life of my own. It wasn't until years later, I realized I never had "girl's day" with girlfriends, gone on a girl's trip, or went anywhere other than work and places I needed to go in order to maintain the home. I decided it was time for me to get a life of my own. I had to figure out besides being a wife and mother what other things I would like to do. I had suppressed who I was for so long in order to be everything to everyone else. One day I discovered, the old "me" was gone, the new "me" was emerging and I started to feel different. My career was one area I needed to change. I felt unfulfilled as a teacher and decided to go back to school.

I enrolled in graduate school and obtained my Master's Degree in Counseling by attending Prairie View A & M, which was an hour and a fifteen minute drive, every Saturday from 8:00-5:00, for three semesters. I would leave home at 6:00 am and get home at 7:00 pm. I went Monday through Friday, for one entire summer, from 8:00 am until 2:00 pm. I was determined to get my degree to progress to another level in my life. I felt if I didn't do something to make changes in my life, I would live a life of contentment like a majority of women; wake up, complain, go to bed, wake up and complain again because they aren't satisfied with their lives. My decision was not to go that route, because my life had more substance. I became a certified school counselor, which was an accomplishment, because I was no longer a teacher. As a counselor, I was still able to impact students, but in a different capacity. Counseling was my niche' or so I thought. The caterpillar in me continued to move her antennas. Ideas were in motion and every day the new woman in me continued to surface.

Once the suppressed woman comes out she realizes that, no matter what, she will fulfill her dreams and allow her visions to become her reality. The dream of a suppressed woman can be a desire to start having "me time" once a month, go back to school to start or finish her degree, change or start a career, leave an unfulfilling relationship, or even start her own business. There may be regret and reservations in her mind that she has waited too long. Ladies, even if you have to wait until the season is right in your life, you must start preparing to follow your dream. It's never too late as Tamar Braxton says, to "Git Yo Life!"

Think About It!

Are you getting a new life, or settling for the life you are living?

We are all faced with opportunities that are dressed up as situations.

CHAPTER

3

Mirror, Mirror
When You Look in the Mirror, How Does the Woman Looking Back at You Feel?

Ladies, I want you to look in the mirror, what do you see, how do you feel? If someone asked you, what you see. Would you talk about your ugly freckles, your eyebrows that need to be waxed, tweezed, threaded, or whatever you do to keep them looking nice, the wrinkle you see today that wasn't there yesterday, the thick lips or broad nose that you are told that you got from your grandmother? Women often compare themselves to the standard the world sets for what is considered beautiful. We look at the things we cannot change about ourselves first, but what we should focus on is the feelings of the woman's reflection looking back at us. Now try the exercise again, is the woman looking back at you satisfied with most aspects of her life? Does she feel happy? Does she have a fulfilling relationship? Does she have a career/job that she wants? Is she satisfied with her level of education? Does she feel that she has reached her full potential? Does she have dreams she wants to accomplish? After doing this exercise, does the feeling about the woman you see change? Do you feel motivated to work on reflections of exercise #1 or #2? We have the ability to change our level of happiness, level of education, relationship status, etc. It's not as easy, if at all possible, without plastic surgery, to change the structure of your face, the size of your nose, remove freckles, or change genetic things about our appearance. Many women focus on what society says we should look like because the focus is outer appearance. As a result many women feel unattractive and walk away feeling like a failure because they do not have the face or body society deems perfect.

It is totally advisable to work on the outer body with exercise, grooming, and eating right. However, many women spend countless hours working on the outer while the inner is being neglected. There are many gorgeous women who appear to have it all, the hair, face, body, the finest jewelry, and clothes, yet they are miserable. They may live very lonely lives because their personality and attitude is so out of whack. People stay away from them, which makes it difficult for them to have true, lasting friendships or relationships.

True beauty comes from within. The amethyst is a stone that comes in various shapes and sizes. The exterior of the stone is not pretty. It's a grainy, brown and rough stone, but when the stone is cracked open it reveals beautiful hues of very smooth purple, pink, and white crystals that sparkle like diamonds. Our lives should reflect that of an amethyst. Our beauty should radiate from the inside out. As we get older, outer beauty fades, but our inner beauty is lasting, it should sparkle and get brighter as we obtain wisdom.

Living life as a smart, sexy, independent, self-confident woman is the best life to have, because those things are never boxed up and put in storage, rather she will take them and make them better. In life, change is evident and constant, as you live, the only thing constant in life is change. Each day life evolves, time waits for no one. Relationships, careers, bodies, beauty, and financial circumstances change.

You have to face change head on in order to become the woman in the mirror you want to be. Step out of your comfort zone and step into new seasons of your life with tenacity. If you are a person who takes baby steps in all that you do, you will always be at a baby stage in your life.

Oftentimes in life we have to step out of our baby shoes, and put on our stilettos. You should not allow yourself to stay in the baby stage too long. Baby steps set you up to stay in your comfort zone, which leads to contentment. Comfort zones can be called "ruts." Many people in their comfort zones are in ruts because they want to move and do something different, but they don't have the motivation to get out. People often think if they are content, they are happy, being content doesn't necessarily mean you are happy.

To move toward happiness allows you to pass a mirror and smile, you must set up a system to achieve the happiness that you want. The first step to creating change within is to be convinced that change is good. If you choose what you are passionate about over what you are comfortable with, change becomes easier. Change should be embraced. Many women are not living the lives they want to live because they are afraid to change the way they think or do things differently. Countless woman go through periods of uncertainty due to fear of the unknown. Some women pretend to be content with their lives, thinking if they change, family and friends will get concerned that something is wrong.

When a woman makes the decision to put herself first and do what pleases her, people around her get uncomfortable because they felt safe and secure when she was predictable. Her sudden independence will raise eyebrows because her behavior is not looked at as a change, but a threat to relationships. Women should not let their happiness be deferred because people around them get uncomfortable. How long have you ignored your comfort and dreams for others? It does not have to be a drastic change it can be a change such as desiring to go back to school, learning a new craft, starting to have girl's night, changing the way you dress, or even changing hairstyles. Family and friends will realize the change may benefit them as well, because you will be a happier person.

In order to be happy with your reflection in the mirror you must make sure your insides are manifesting what you want people to see on the outside. Imagination can take you to reality if you focus on what's in your heart and continue to make steps and watch your dream develop.

I attribute appreciation of my reflection to the shedding of my cocoon and starting my emergence as a caterpillar. I have always had a wonderful bond with my daughters; my goal as a mother was to be a role model for them. I wanted them to be successful, independent women. I taught them and modeled necessary things they needed to stand out as young ladies. They were taught to do laundry, cook, bake, keep a clean house, do their nails, feet and hair, they also learned different crafts. I was an avid reader; thankfully they both picked up that trait and enjoyed reading. We would look forward to weekends to go to the bookstore. Some young girls and teens would find going to the bookstore boring, they found it fun and exciting. Knowledge has always been a symbol of power, only if you apply it. I wanted them to be well-rounded women; however, I felt that if I stressed independence and success I had to demonstrate that as well. As they transitioned from young ladies to teens, they saw me juggle many tasks and remain organized in order to keep our home calm. I remember looking at my reflection in the mirror, wondering how was I able to do all I had to do on a daily basis.

My husband was rarely home, he was a hard worker who spent lots of long hours working to provide for us. I demonstrated to my daughters how to keep the home in order in the absence of their father. The girls and I had schedules for everything, chores and schoolwork first, but we always made time for fun. As they grew older our home became the home where their friends would like to come to spend the weekend. We were always doing something that interested their friends, we would cook, bake, do crafty projects, play beauty shop in the kitchen, and we would play our favorite game Scrabble. We enjoyed life, bonding as mother and daughters. Although, I felt I was setting examples from the things I did, I still felt that I was stressing independence and being successful, yet I was dependent upon their father to provide. Being a provider is the primary role of the man of the house; however, I always felt that women should have a level of independence. There are women I know who do not know the first thing to do to check the oil levels in their car, get their oil changed, check the air pressure in their tires, or even put gas in their cars. I am not saying that it's something wrong if your partner does all those things for you, but at least know what to do if you have to. My husband had two back surgeries and a heart attack; therefore I was fortunate that I knew how to hold things together while he was recovering. My reflection in the mirror started to change as my daughters got older.

When my oldest daughter was a sophomore in high school, I decided to substitute teach because I felt that being a teacher would be a good career for me. I wanted to get hands-on experience before I committed to enroll in college. I thought education was important and seeing how many students lacked interest in education, I wanted to make a difference. There were perks to becoming a teacher. I would be able to work the same hours my daughters were at school, after school we would be home at the same time, also I would get to spend summers and holiday's with them. My goal was to obtain my degree before my oldest daughter graduated high school. My daughters were older, therefore, I felt it would be easier to go to school, and juggle responsibilities as a wife and mother. I continued to substitute two days a week and attended college three days a week.

Things were going smoothly; I was scheduled to graduate in December, my daughter in May. In September, my husband was injured at work, which resulted in a back injury. I had to stop subbing to care for him. His injury caused excruciating pain, which kept us up all night. He couldn't walk, I had to help him shower, brush his teeth, literally care for him, in addition to going to school. I had come too far to turn back. I would care for him and make sure he had what he needed before I went to school. My neighbor would come and check on him while I was at school. Once the girls and I got home it was time for dinner. Thank God they were able to help out a lot with chores because they were taught what to do at an early age. I remember helping them with assignments, taking care of my husband, taking a shower, going to bed about 10:00 or 11:00 and setting the clock for midnight, I would study until 3:00 or 4:00 am. I would go to bed for two hours and start my day all over again. The injury caused so much pain and discomfort that he had to have back surgery in November. After the surgery, I had to care for the wound, do his back treatments with this special machine and give meds on time, I became a nurse overnight. I still managed to spend time with my daughters to make sure they were not neglected. They helped out with their dad as much as they could. However, being girls there were things they were not able to help with.

In addition to being a nurse, mother, and wife, I had my student hat to wear, so I had to schedule time to study for finals. Being a month away from graduation, I was determined not to give up. My independence and duty as a wife did not allow the thought to ask for help from family or friends to cross my mind. The new responsibilities came naturally. Although, it was a difficult time, with prayer, perseverance and wonderful daughters, I was able to finish the semester! I graduated, with honors and was able to participate in the ceremony. Initially, I thought due to my husband's surgery I wouldn't be able to attend the ceremony. He said because of my sacrifices and dedication to my roles during his recovery, he was going even if he had to crawl. He was able to walk slowly on a cane, but we made it! There were days I felt like giving up, but I kept my eyes on the prize and focused on my goal. I knew the storm wouldn't last forever. I made a decision that I would not be defeated. By no means did I think I was Superwoman, but I did what I had to.

In life, there is freedom and choice to have a good or bad day. You are the author of your life. Every day you write a chapter in your life story. You have to take responsibility for who you are and who you want to be. What you think and how you feel will determine what you do. Human nature has conditioned us to feel safe to do what we are familiar with rather than step out and walk into the unknown; we have to walk in our own shoes to be comfortable.

The next time you look in a mirror, will you frown, smile, or embrace the woman that looks back at you? If you start now making changes within to be happy, the mirror won't intimidate you and regret will not follow you from one season of your life to the next.

Most people say, "Life is too, short." My theory, as an optimist is, "Life is too long to be dissatisfied."

In order to have a fulfilling life inside and out you have to make changes. "If you do things the same way you've always done, you get the results you've always gotten," so change is good! A good way to think about change is to daily hum the tune, of *Man in the Mirror* by the late Michael Jackson, "I'm starting with the [wo]man in the mirror, I'm asking [her] to change [her]way."

Think About It
What is the face saying that's looking at you when you look in the mirror?

If there wasn't a way to
get over life's problems,
they would not be called hurdles.
Sometimes in life you have to put your
track shoes on.

CHAPTER

4

Where Is My GPS?
Follow the Yellow Brick Road

You can't change the past to start a new beginning, but you can start today to begin a new ending. In order to live the life you have dreamed of you have to be confident and walk in the direction of your dreams, but most of us do not know which direction to take. How often have you asked yourself, "Where do I go from here?" Sometimes in life we wonder if our path has gotten crossed with someone else's or we ask ourselves, "When did I get off course?" Wouldn't it be wonderful if our lives had a Guidance Pointing System or GPS? If we did, we could plug in where we are and where we want to go. The GPS would suggest different routes, as well as, tell us how long it would take to arrive at our destination. We would be offered shortcuts. Today's society has been spoiled by the conveniences of technology. We no longer have to use landmarks, pen and paper, make several phones calls, or use post it notes to get directions to find our destination. You can simply type in your current location and arrival destination into your phone, Google maps, MapQuest, etc. and voila you are there! Unfortunately, life doesn't come with a GPS. The paths we travel are learned by trial and error.

Most mistakes we make in life can be avoided. However, as human beings, some lessons aren't truly learned and do not stick in our mind until we have experienced an uncomfortable situation, which causes the event to stay with us forever. There are some people who continue to make the same mistakes. Our happiness has a lot to do with our circumstances, based on what we think and do on a daily basis. As women, we are so busy we often lose sight of our goals and dreams.

Life requires patience and willingness in order to be content where you are in your life while you wait on something better. Sometimes in the race of life trying to get from one point to the next, you feel worn out. But with persistence, you can reach your goal. For contentment to take place, you must have a mind and heart of gratitude. Gratitude is often our guide. You will be empowered when you recognize that in spite of not being at the point in your life where you want to be, you have to focus on the blessings you do have. Think about your blessings. What if they were taken away? Your life course would then take a different direction. Focus on what you have and stop focusing on what you don't have. Be patient until your life is steered in the direction for your personal journey. Everyone's GPS of life has a different course, so the paths we take will not all lead to the same destination. Just because you are born a female, doesn't mean you will have the same life path as Michelle Obama, Oprah Winfrey, Beyoncé, Hillary Clinton, Claire Huxtable, or the famous television housewife of the 70's, June Cleaver. June did her daily chores without a hint of stress while wearing her beautiful dresses and pearls. June's life did not depict the life of a true housewife. I am sure all of these women encountered detours and had to take short cuts in order to get to their destination. No one can see behind the scenes of what life is really like for these women. What we see is the outcome, which is glitz and glamour. We all have a different path. We may not end up rich and famous, but it doesn't mean we can't.

Sometimes we may wonder when our life path will straighten out because surely this isn't the life we ordered. Opportunities are missed when you focus too much on the future. The opportunities that are right before your eyes can be overlooked if you are looking too far ahead. Embrace the present and make the most out of it now. Notice and celebrate things that you have accomplished. You do not have to wait until your desired goal is reached. There are times in life when we have to trust God to give us the peace to continue on our journey until our path is lined out. In order for us to be grateful for what we have, we must look for something good in all situations. Without warning, fear and doubt can creep in and crowd your mind with negative thoughts or images. *"What if I never get my bills paid?"* *"What if I never get a new house?"* *"What if I stay in this unfulfilling relationship?"* The "what if" syndrome has stopped many people from being happy and what manifests in their lives is what they are focused on, the "what if's."

Even when things seem impossible, you have to believe and have faith that success is right around the corner. Holding on to your desires and dreams should be your focus rather than what is not going as planned. When your mind takes a detour and pulls up to the street of negative *what if's*, pull over, reroute, and change your path to positive "what if's." "What if I get the job I want?" What if I get the house I want?" There are ways to turn negative words into positive affirmations. You have to keep your direction in mind. Although our minds are not as easy to program as a GPS, we have direction, it is called choice. Choose to go down the positive road if your mind's GPS is leading you to a negative place, you can always reroute, it takes practice. Anything that you desire to perfect in life, takes practice. "For a dream comes through much activity, and a fool's voice is known by his many words." Ecclesiastes 5:3 NKJV. This profound verse simply states that you have to work on your dream for it to become a reality. You can talk about what you want all day, but if you don't put it into action, it will never manifest.

You cannot reach your goals and dreams by just

thinking about them, you must take action. You reach your dreams by doing what it takes to make them happen. Stepping towards your dream may cause discomfort, because you are taken out of your comfort zone, but sitting idle is like watching your dream pass you by. Making your dreams come true starts with you. What are your dreams? What are you willing to do to make your dreams come true? In the end, your decision to fulfill your dreams begins and ends with you. My father used to tell my sister's and me, "Nothing comes to a sleeper, but a dream." We never understood the meaning until we got older. In order to make your dreams come true, you have to wake up from your dream and take action. Procrastinating will cause stress and much disappointment when you have a goal in mind. Procrastination will take longer for you to reach your goal, because it wastes time and energy.

At the age of 19, I had been married for a year and was pregnant with my first child. I did not have a dream or know what I wanted to do because I was content being a housewife and soon to be mother. Although I was encouraged by my husband to enroll in a community college, I had no desire to attend because I had no particular career interest. I was being taken care of, my needs were met, why would I want to leave my content place to venture into the unknown? I continued to take care of my duties as a wife. Shortly after, I had duties of being a new mother. Still in the protective shield of my cocoon, I was content with my life.

Once my daughter was about eight months old, I decided I would enroll in college. I attended two semesters. It was very difficult caring for a young baby, being a wife, and attending college. I did not enroll a third semester. Every day I would think to myself, "I should have stuck with it." I procrastinated on and off for a few years, then finally went on to get my associates degree. It took me four years; which is equivalent to the time it takes to get a bachelor's degree.

Shortly after, I became pregnant with my second daughter. I worked a few jobs as an administrative assistant, but was never content. I did not have a passion for anything in particular, so I just went day-to-day, not knowing what I wanted to do other then be a role model for my daughters.

We can change the direction or course of our lives, with God's permission and guidance. We must be willing to face obstacles and challenges. After all, the Creator of the Universe has the GPS for our lives. We just don't know which direction He will present before us. This is the time where we have to flex our faith muscles; we don't have to know all of the answers. The true meaning of trusting God, is being comfortable while we wait on our instructions. We have to ask ourselves, "Even though I do not know where my dream will take me, am I ready to embrace change?" Change is a complex process, we either decide to make the change or change comes to us unexpectedly. The outcome is determined by the way we handle change. Our decisions ultimately shape the outcome of our destiny. If we focus on the directions given to us on our personal GPS, our final destination will be exactly where we are supposed to be.

Jamie's Story

Jamie grew up in an abusive household that left her with false perceptions of love and fulfilling relationships. The abuse she witnessed left emotional scars, which caused her to have a difficult time building relationships with the opposite sex. As a young woman, she always chose a partner similar to her father, but that was never her intent. After several failed relationships throughout high school, in college she found what she thought was the man of her dreams; he was "different from all the rest." During the course of their two-year relationship, she witnessed he had a temper and would explode at things she felt was not a big deal. Deep inside she felt his temper was similar to her father's, but Alan was not an alcoholic. She felt she could deal with his temper. After all, his outbursts were never directed towards her. She did not want to be alone. After much thought, she looked back on previous relationships of family and friends and realized there were no perfect relationships. She felt that all relationships would take work. Although friends and family noticed his subtle ways, Alan showed he wasn't the mild mannered guy Jamie said he was. After dating for three and a half years and finishing college as a business major, Jamie married Alan.

Within the first two months of marriage. Jamie noticed Alan began to show his hostility and anger towards her. This was a side of him that she had not noticed while dating. The hostility got worse during the first year of their marriage. However, Jamie was too embarrassed to let her friends or family members know the secret she was living with because they questioned his temper prior to the marriage. She did not want a failed marriage and the cycle of abuse continued.

One night at a birthday celebration for one of her coworkers, things did not go as she planned. Jamie baked a beautiful cake, baking had become her passion and escape from frustration with the marriage. Someone made a comment about her talent of cake decorating. Alan made several negative comments out loud about her talent not being that great to him. Jamie ignored him, which made him very angry. As a result, Alan yelled at her in front of her coworkers, which was a total embarrassment. At this point, Jamie was done. She made a decision that night to leave. She was also thankful that she had no children. She was smart enough to know that she could not just go home, pack her things, and leave. She needed courage and a plan of escape. She started looking into new jobs, places to relocate, saving money, and establishing credit of her own. It took her five months of enduring the pain and abuse before she was able to make her escape.

Jamie succeeded in divorcing Alan. She found a less stressful, higher paying job in another city. Once Jamie was settled into her new life, she decided it was time to pursue her dream. She pursued her dream of having her own bakery, because she loved to bake and would often admire her beautiful cakes. Jamie's business became so successful; she was booked for weddings, anniversaries, birthday celebrations, and it eventually afforded her the opportunity to quit her full time job. People admired the uniqueness of her decorating style. She had never been happier making a living. She was finally making money, doing what she loved.

Today, Jamie is married to the man of her dreams, has two children, and has opened her third bakery.

When our GPS gets re-routed, it often leads us on a path to happiness. We must take risk and not settle for an unfulfilling life. Remember, contentment does not mean happiness.

Think About It
Have you had to re-route your GPS to guide you in the right direction?

PART

2

The Caterpillar Stage

During the caterpillar stage, the cocoon has been unwrapped. It goes through metamorphosis to prepare the butterfly for its debut. However, the caterpillar has to be nurtured and allowed to grow in order for the butterfly to emerge. The caterpillar spends most of its time eating and absorbing nutrients. As women in the caterpillar stage, we are absorbing information, learning what we like, deciding who we are, and what we want to do. We are hungry for adventure. It appears the caterpillar stage is when many women have an awakening.

Women often realize at this point that they have new interest; there are certain hobbies, places, people, and things that no longer feel comfortable or fit in their lives. This is the time women often feel they have outgrown the skin they are in. However, many women get stuck in the caterpillar stage due to fear of change. They feel it's too late to fulfill their dreams and live out their desires because of obligations such as family, career, or lack of motivation.

Metamorphosis is when the caterpillar goes through a major transformation. Unfortunately, many women never progress from a caterpillar because they allow their limits to keep them content with living the life that they have been living; even if they aren't happy. Although there are women who totally reinvent themselves and do not allow anything or anyone stop them. The cocoon has been shed, the caterpillar has emerged. Have you ever felt the need to make changes in your life to experience new things because the old things don't have a place in your life anymore? Give yourself permission to step out of your cocoon.

"People cry, not because
they're weak. It's because
they've been strong for too long."-
Johnny Depp

CHAPTER
5

Be Yourself, Everyone Else is Taken
"As we grow as unique persons, we learn to respect the uniqueness of others."-Robert H. Schuller

In today's society, many women want the life of other women, whether it's to be a size five, have a different length or type of hair, a toned body, financial status, or the idea of a perfect relationship. Women who are admired by others also have role models or someone they would change places with. It is human nature, to want what we don't have or be who we are not. God made each of us unique. Rather than take our uniqueness and work with it, we often try to imitate others in order to feel complete. We all must develop and use our special gifts each day to learn things that are valuable to our personal growth.

Each time we celebrate a birthday new challenges come along with the new year. As we get older, we learn to appreciate who we are and accept ourselves exactly the way we are. Getting older puts our focus in a different direction. We are more concerned with our health and wellness than with the latest hairstyles, fashions, and who's who. We notice our body is changing, beauty fading, and our thoughts shifting from what we once thought were important. Since change is constant, we are always going to be presented with challenges.

Challenges often cause us to want to escape from our current life to avoid focusing on the things that cause discomfort. We try to escape all the woulda, coulda, shouldas.

Sometimes we get trapped by our thoughts of not being that "perfect" woman. Thoughts often cross our minds like, *If only I had Oprah's money, Kim Kardashian's body, Beyoncé's personality and fame, or a relationship with our partner like President Barack and Michelle Obama.* At some point we have to end our pity parties and live our lives according to the blueprint we were given. Oftentimes, jealousy, envy, or pure sadness can cause women to be unproductive in their lives because they are stuck in someone else's life. Rather than letting your life pass by while other women are being productive, you have to make a conscience decision to get out of your rut, take the power, and be who you were designed to be. The image you have of yourself affects many parts of your life. The first step is to appreciate you for who you are. Remember, the opinion others have of you is none of your business. What is important is what you think of yourself.

As I started my evolvement from a caterpillar to a butterfly, I knew it was time for me to soar to new heights. I remember growing up watching my mother settle and be content with her life. She often said, "I didn't have the opportunities that you all have today." My mother was very popular in school, but as she grew older she had fewer friends that she would talk to. My mother was very friendly and would help anyone, but she was more of a loner. She didn't have a lot of visitors and she rarely visited anyone. My mother sewed on occasion, but she did not have any hobbies or a life outside of our family. Although she was not happy, she became content with her job. She continued to go every day and never looked for options to do more. She would say to us, "don't do as I did, get your education." My mother had a high school education, which only allowed her to be employed in positions that paid minimal salaries.

I observed her life and realized life had more to offer. She deserved it, but did not seek anything different. As I became a young woman, I decided to look further into what I could do to have a different life rather than settle into a life of contentment. I always felt there was someone inside of me trying to get out but I ignored the nudge and the still voice that said, "I have the power to be whatever I want to be." Ideas would come to my mind and I would say, "Nah, that's not what I want to do." I did not give up. I continued to search my mind and heart with prayer and determination, which allowed me to focus on doing something that, would be a job, but not feel like a job.

During the journey to self-discovery you must be around people who will lift you up, you must stay positive, focused and research ways to learn things on your journey. Your body, mind, and spirit need to be enriched. You have to find the strength to gain a new perspective of who you are, what you want, and where you want to be.

You must ask yourself a very powerful question, "How can I be the best me that I can be?" You must put on your mental workout clothes and hit the ground running. While you are getting dressed for your new journey, you must keep in mind that as you get older, you can't take baby steps. You have enough knowledge and wisdom to take leaps and tackle the change head-on. Once you get started with your journey to self-discovery realize that you have to learn how to think outside the box. You are unique; you will begin to see your dreams come true. As a matter of fact, if we would get rid of the box, we would have a major mission accomplished. If the box isn't there, you can't get back in when you feel insecure. You will have no choice but to take steps toward your goal.

Next, ask yourself, "What are my dreams? What am I willing to do to see my dreams come true?" Each of our journeys are determined by our decisions. There are changes we make consciously, like changing careers, going back to school, relocating, letting go of relationships or friendships that are hindering our growth, losing weight, and many other decisions we make consciously. Even when unexpected changes come, loss of employment, divorce, illness, the outcome of who we become and how we embrace change is solely up to us. The decisions we make in life shape our destiny. As Audrey Hepburn once said, "I believe that happy girls are the prettiest girls." Happiness shows from the inside out.

You must truly discover that you are a "diva" within and must know the self-worth you were born with. The perceptions of others can often change how we feel about ourselves; it isn't what you wear, how you wear your hair, what you do for a living or the accessories you accent with. True beauty comes from within. Self-confidence can create a glow within you that radiates around you. You can walk into a room and without saying a word, and release confidence that cannot be purchased, it must be developed within yourself.

As time goes on, life happens and the glow you once had gets dull and needs polishing. Life experiences can cause your self-worth to fade little by little. Once your self-worth starts to fade, you start looking at the lives of others and daydreaming about having a different life. As we get older, life can be mundane and you start to get bored and restless. You must then look inside of your heart and soul to tap into the beauty of who you are within. The minute you realize you were born to live a joyful, happy, and peaceful life, nothing can dim your light. You will have a glow that cannot be dulled.

Every morning and throughout the day, you should look in the mirror and say, "I Love the Me I See. There is No One Else I'd Rather Be!"

Think About It!
Are you being yourself or wishing you could trade places and be someone else?

Be good to yourself, you only
get one life. Stay positive, stay
focused, and don't let people or
circumstances dictate your destiny.

CHAPTER

6

Do you have what it takes to be the woman of HIS dreams?

"The Sexiest Thing a Woman Can Wear is Confidence"

How do you know if you are the right woman? Do you have the characteristics and dedication to be the woman of a man's dreams? Many women think being single is a sad state to be in, therefore they settle for unhealthy or unfulfilling relationships for the sake of being with someone, not realizing it is better to be single than in the wrong relationship. Men want women in their lives who will bring something to the relationship and will allow them to become a better man. A man's dream is to have a confident woman by his side. They want a woman who knows who she is and what she wants. Women must take time to know and love themselves before they are able to be a partner in a loving relationship. The mistake that women often make is trying to change who they are to be what they think the man is looking for, rather than being themselves. It is best to be yourself at all times, because sooner or later the real you will come out. Hiding who you are can cause conflicts in relationships because you will begin to do things that are not natural and the real personality will eventually surface.

This chapter isn't to tell women they have to be doormats in order to be a partner. It is also not saying that men are perfect and do not have to be committed and make sacrifices as well. It is simply to offer tools and insight to evaluating whether or not you are ready to take the steps to be the woman of some man's dreams. As a seasoned woman in a long-term marriage, I have spoken to many women both single and married who are unhappy. They wonder why their relationships do not last, or they say there are "not any good men left." There are many single and married women who do not want to make the sacrifices to do what it takes to be in a committed relationship. It is by far an easy task, but it can be done. For instance, many women settle into their comfort zones once they feel they have their partner's attention, they forget about the little things they did to get him. If he was attracted to you because he liked your appearance, or how you cooked his favorite meals and baked his favorite desserts; once you get comfortable don't stop doing those things. Whatever you did to get him you must continue doing those things to keep him. If you were available for intimacy at his beck and call initially, you can't a get "headache" or say you don't feel good five out of seven days because now you are "tired." Relationships usually start off great, each person going the extra mile to please the other. Couples often notice things that make them uncomfortable at the beginning, but fail to say anything for fear they may cause an argument or discord. There are often red flags in new relationships that go unnoticed because of the hope the person will "change." Dr. Maya Angelou said it best, "When a person shows you who they are, believe them."

Men are physical by nature; they are attracted to a woman's outer appearance. When a man looks at his woman he doesn't want the image of his grandmother when he goes to bed. How appealing is it to a man to get in bed and rollover to his woman with her head in a bonnet, scarf, or "rag?" Her night attire is a big tee shirt, old workout shorts, or a cotton gown with Garfield or a Disney character on the front that she's had for several years. The colors are no longer vibrant they are now dull and thin. After a hard day at work, a man wants to come home to look at a sexy woman. It can be something as simple as a pair of short, shorts, with a sexy top, nice lingerie, or nothing at all with a pair of stilettos. Women you know your man and what he likes, so every now and again, surprise him and do something special for him. Don't wait until he complains or has to ask you to do something special. There are days you may be tired and do not feel like being sexy, but it takes the same time to put on lingerie as it does any other night attire. Just the look of a sexy woman can be enough to put your man in a great mood. He will appreciate the effort you took. Men like spontaneity and embrace times when their woman initiates intimacy. Of course there will be times that you may not feel up to being sexy, but the outcome of pleasing your man is worth it. There are seven days in a week, if you dedicate two or three to just wearing a special outfit, high heel shoes, cooking his favorite meal, or planning a night of intimacy, your man will adore you. Some men don't require all the bells and whistles, they will just be happy to come home and your hair isn't wrapped up, or you are wearing a comfortable sundress as opposed to your old worn out robe. It's not always the big things; the small things can speak volumes.

New relationships are easy because of the excitement, expectations, and adventure. There are many couples that have issues from the beginning, but they ignore them. When getting to know someone during conversations, you learn their interests. Sometimes, people are in such a hurry for a relationship they fail to see warning signs that the relationship may not be the best one for them. Here are a few common scenarios:

- Women, if you meet a guy and he says that he likes horses and going to the rodeo, why would you pursue the relationship if you know that you will never go near a horse and cannot stomach the smell at the rodeo? Yet, you can clearly see while in the "get to know you" stage that he has a passion for horses.

- You meet a guy at the gas station on a motorcycle, you exchange numbers, hang out a few times, all he talks about is his motorcycle, the next motorcycle rally, or you constantly see and hear him purchasing accessories for his "bike." You tell your girlfriend you are afraid of motorcycles and will never ride on it....why get involved with a passionate biker from the beginning? Do you think he will park his motorcycle in the garage or sell it because of you? Eventually, he will want you to accompany him on his bike, if you blatantly refuse or act totally disinterested in his biker activities, don't get upset when he goes without you, or has someone else riding with him. If you are afraid to ride on the bike, buy him an accessory, drive your own vehicle to the biker rally. Be involved!

- You are introduced to a guy in the grocery store, it's obvious, by the looks of his body that he faithfully attends the gym. You can tell he doesn't go to the gym only to look at the equipment. By the items in his basket, you notice that he eats healthy and drinks lots of water. Eventually, he may invite you to workout with him, or encourage you to do some form of exercise. Don't get upset because you, hate working out, can't afford to sweat out your hair, or you feel like he's criticizing your body. When you met him, he had a body of a Greek god. Buy a couple of workout outfits, go to the gym with him a few times, and find healthy recipes to cook. Get involved!

- Let's not forget the guy you meet in the parking lot with his Texans football jersey, Texans baseball cap, and a Texan's sticker in the rear window of his truck. Are these all signs that he just might be a sports fan? Why get upset because all he wants to do is watch football every chance he gets? Sit beside him and learn the sport, fix nachos or some type of concession stand snack, occasionally enjoy the game with him.

- Finally, you meet a guy who is divorced with a few children; you have never been married and don't have any children. The guy tells you up front that he does not want a commitment or any children… if you know you wish to be married and have children…please leave that man alone! You are only setting yourself up for future disappointment.

As stated earlier, many people know what they are getting when beginning a relationship, but the things that bother you are ignored. If you meet a guy and he tells you his interest, if you are not interested in the least you are wasting your time and his. However, if you enter a relationship with a willing heart and open mind, you will overcome many obstacles and have minimal conflicts. If there is something you know you WILL NOT do, then move on to someone more compatible. You can't change someone who had passions and a certain interest when you met him. If you show interest sometime, the times you don't will be okay, because he feels satisfied that you are not totally disinterested in what he likes to do.

Conflicts in relationships are often created because couples do not do what it takes to make one another happy. Relationships often end due to conflicts that are not resolved because of lack of communication. Couples often hurt each other without realizing they are causing emotional pain. Emotional needs are very important and are often the needs that are most neglected. Men and women should understand and appreciate the needs of one another, but often fail in this area. The needs of men and women are very different. Couples often fail at satisfying needs because they try to meet the wrong needs. In order to make one another happy you must be aware of the emotional needs and learn to meet those. Feelings are often taking for granted until it's too late. For instance, if your partner is going through a family or employment situation, he may not be able to express himself emotionally. You can support him emotionally by holding him, sitting quietly next to him, giving him a gentle kiss, or letting him know that you are there for him when he feels like discussing the matter. Whatever you do, do not badger him to talk, it will add to frustration. If you know your partner does not like to talk immediately when a situation arises and you bombard him the minute he walks through the door or calls you, that behavior, causes an additional conflict to make the initial conflict worse. Women often call that communicating, men call it nagging. Couples must learn to communicate and learn to meet the needs of the other person. Successful relationships require skill, patience, and communication. Modeled behavior is the best way to show your partner how to meet your needs.

Expectations are high when relationships are developing, but many people believe in order to have a successful relationship the 50/50 rule must be applied. Actually each person in the relationship should give 100%. The way to keep a relationship happy is to prioritize things that important to your partner. It may be important for a man to have quiet time and it may be important for a woman to be complimented, each need is important to the other person and must be met in order for the person to be fulfilled.

As women we are emotional beings, we like to communicate, be complimented, receive gifts, and to be treated like we are the only thing that matters to our man. If you do not want to go the extra mile to meet his needs the relationship will be one-sided. Women often think, *"Why should I have to give and he doesn't?"* Women and men often look at needs the opposite way. It is often a matter of communication and paying attention to behaviors. Couples are willing to please, but what one person thinks is important, the other person thinks it's not.

It's important for a man to know his woman is beautiful inside and out. Outer beauty can be the way the woman carries herself. She keeps her hair intact, nails and feet manicured, eyebrows tamed, takes pride in her body, and she is classy and confident. Inner beauty is of utmost importance, personality plays a big part in relationships on both sides. Men want their women to be approachable, just as women want their men to be approachable. Introducing your mate, who has a rude, unapproachable personality to a co-worker, former classmate, or relative, is uncomfortable and embarrassing. If you want your mate to adore you make sure you are adorable, inside and out.

There are characteristics men look for in a good woman. Being a good communicator is the foundation of a relationship. Without communication there is no relationship. It cannot be stressed enough; communication is the key to a healthy successful relationship. However, the foundation is important, but for the building to stand you must have a frame to build around.

1. **Confidence**- A confident woman is very appealing to a man. A woman that accepts her imperfections and is not afraid to be herself, she is confident and proud of who she is.

2. **Supportive**- A supportive woman will be there for her man mentally, emotionally, and physically. You must be a good listener, comforter, and allow your man the freedom to show emotions and still let him know that he is strong in your eyes. If he wants to talk about work, allow him to vent, you must be there to provide the comfort he needs.

3. **Independent**- To a man, an independent woman demonstrates her ability to manage and take care of

herself. Men want to be providers, not babysitters. Independent women can stand on their own two feet and take care of business if their partner can't be there. However, women should not be too independent because men feel they are not needed. Men want to feel needed, but like a level of independence in a woman.

4. **Loyalty**- Men want to feel that no matter what their woman will be by their side. When the going gets tough a loyal woman will stick by her man's side and face the situation together.

5. **Status**- A man wants to know that his woman loves him and wants to be with him because of the man he is, not the status he holds. Money and status can buy love, but love that comes from the heart will last for a lifetime.

6. **Humble**- Men prefer modest and humble women as opposed to high maintenance, snobbish women, who often put more into their appearance and what the man can give them then they do their feelings for the man or the relationship.

7. **Discrete**- Women who gossip and tell every detail of their relationship to friends, family, and others are often a turnoff to a man because he looks like the bad guy because of what has been said about him regarding the relationship.

8. **Well-Rounded**- A man likes a woman that can get along with his family and friends, she likes things he likes, and can be spontaneous.

Several men ages 30-55 (some were married, single, divorced, or dating) were asked various questions regarding the quality of a woman they would date, importance of education, communication, pet peeves, what they like and don't like for women to do, or personalities that are favored:

- "Depends on what the man wants and desires. Some men would take the dumbest woman with the biggest butt and make her smart. Some men would take a woman who is very intelligent, but not the most beautiful woman, and make her his jewel. All women are emotional in some way. A man has to decide whether he can deal with what he has chosen, as far as emotions go. Most women cry and wear their hearts on their sleeves, while other women may hide their emotions. Me, if they hide emotions, I'm running… Now, as far as physical, I want curves and all men do. That's the nature of the man. I feel a woman should be soft and smooth while some men prefer hard bodied women. Men are mysterious creatures and you may never know why a man likes what he likes. Hell, half of the time he doesn't know why. It's something in this mysterious world that drives a man's desires, wants, and preferences."

- "An ideal relationship wouldn't look like an ice cream cone on a hot sunny day. I say that because in order to have an ideal relationship, means logically and respectfully working through those differences and obstacles. An ideal relationship means that you don't mind adapting to whatever differences you have with our partner. You're compatible; you have similar ideas, YES. Even though, some couples are totally different, the key to survival for those couples are open minds, good listeners, good heart, desire to learn new things, accept new behaviors etc… Ideal relationships don't always look like gold, you have to polish them."

- "The key to an ideal relationship is definitely to be fair across the board, needs and wants! The great hierarchy is it looks good on paper, the 50/50, but only on paper. My thoughts are we say that's what we want; however, the reality is that's what we strive for. Humans are selfish beings, we want what we want. We are people of takers, but some are just willing to share more or compromise because it's just in their nature to give more. The scales are usually unbalanced; the key is finding the right ingredient."

- "Expectations are for a woman "To be all you can be" in the truest sense. A woman must be able to be a chameleon, adapting to her environment. Negativity is a big NO!! Education is very; very important... However, the measuring stick of an intellect is not just for the degreed because sometimes they are too smart for their own good. Our existence depends on education. Ignorance is bliss. A woman must have the willingness to learn. A turn off is an UNORGANIZED, SLOPPY, loud mouth, and women who make excuses for their shortcomings. Things that were important in my 20s and 30s is different now that I am in my 40s; granted, the basic premise is the same. My maturity has altered what is ideal now. Beauty and not brains is like eating chitterlings and pancakes, it just doesn't work. I want a woman that is a helpmate and not straddle the fence. Don't claim independence if you're not independent. Support your man; be able to agree to disagree when there is healthy dialog. African American women are particularly strong. Their endurance, strength and stamina is unparalleled."

- "I think the most important thing one must do is identify who they are and write out a list of things that are important [to them]. Couples should make a list of expectations of what they are looking for; however leave room for flexibility and error. No one is perfect. We chose to have a mate but don't take the time to pray to God and ask him to send him or her to us."

- "Every man wants a woman they can come home to and to be real with. They want to come home to their best friend, not a nagging woman dressed like their grandmother with headscarves on, and granny gowns. Men want to come home and be treated like a King, have a clean house, and a home cooked meal on occasion if the woman works outside the home. Men want to know they are doing a good job as a mate. They need to hear praise from their woman

All good relationships are based on mutual respect. If you do not feel respect for your partner, or believe your partner does not have respect for you, then consider ways of rebuilding, or discontinuing the relationship immediately. Respect is the key. If you have true respect for one another, you will achieve the goals you are reaching for in your relationship.

Think About It!
Do you have what it takes to be a confident woman?

If you try something 99 times and succeed one time, think of the 99 times as practice.

CHAPTER

7

What Is the Butterfly Effect?

"Just when the caterpillar thought the world was over, it became a butterfly."-Proverb

There are many women, who like the caterpillar, feel as if they have come to a dead end in their lives. If you look deeply into the quote above, you realize it speaks of new beginnings that create a different perspective of life. When we were born, we started out as babies. We had to learn to crawl, walk, and later we learned to run. Of course, our life cycle is much longer then the caterpillar's and involves more than a metamorphosis. Whether we emerge into a beautiful fluttering butterfly or not, depends on how we accept the stages of change in our lives.

Butterflies symbolize freedom, hope, joy, and new beginnings. Each of these are also symbols of rebirth, out with the old, in with the new. In life, we must go through several stages of development before our true purpose is revealed. Some women have kept their cocoon wrapped tightly around their lives and hearts. They have not allowed opportunities, to create new experiences, to love, grow, and develop into the person they truly should be. We must break out of our comfort zone, which is equivalent to our cocoon, in order to experience a new beginning; which is our flight as a butterfly.

For several reasons, butterflies symbolize femininity. A woman's graceful walk compares to a soaring butterfly gliding through the sky. The colors of the beautiful wings are symbols of a woman, her outer beauty radiating from inside out. Beauty and grace are qualities that women and butterflies share. Butterflies, like women, transform in stages. Some progress quickly, some progress slowly, and others get stuck in an uncertain stage. But once they break through the stage, they emerge and evolve as a graceful beautiful butterfly. Women have unique flight patterns, just as the butterfly. We are all unique in our thoughts, dreams, and goals.

Butterflies are known as beautiful insects that soar in the air, usually during the spring. Most people don't realize the beauty and uniqueness of each one. The symbol of a butterfly is very powerful as it represents emerging and evolving. A women's life can be compared to the stages of a butterfly. The **moth** stage, is compared to the life of a human from infancy to early teens, this is considered the molding stage. The **cocoon** is the stage of protection and exploration. As a cocoon, young ladies are trying to find their niche, style, choose friends, and interest, all while parents and adults who are a part of their lives are still protecting them. The **caterpillar** is the breakaway stage when the woman starts to shed her cocoon. She's no longer protected by the innocence of not knowing right from wrong and is now responsible for her actions. Many women get to the caterpillar stage and either blossom, or they get stuck. As a butterfly a woman emerges and evolves. She knows who she is, what she wants, and will soar to great heights to achieve her dream. Becoming a butterfly is a peaceful fearless time of a woman's life. However, women often get so focused on living their life; they forget to love life. They often spend so much of their time taking care of the needs of others; they get stuck in a stage of a cocoon or caterpillar and never experience a fulfilled life. This causes many women to be on an endless search for their dream.

I was an example of a woman who stayed in her cocoon for an extended period of time. I got married at the age of 18. While my classmates were sending out graduation invitations, I was sending out wedding invitations. I was still in my cocoon because I was protected and covered by my parents, leaving their protection, going directly into the protection of a husband, and becoming a wife one month after high school graduation.

Seeking wisdom always came to me naturally. My idea of an average week as a high school student was spending time during the afternoon visiting my paternal grandmother, Big Mama and several of the elderly women in my neighborhood. I also spent weekends with my maternal grandmother, Hannah Lee, and maternal great grandmother, Granny. I would sit for hours and talk to them about life and experiences they had. It amazed me how entertaining it was to sit and listen to their stories because I was learning valuable life lessons. It may sound odd, but I was more interested in learning to crochet, do embroidery, sew, bake and learn about the Bible than spend time with teens my age. It was interesting how things were different for me as a teenage compared to when they were teens. I wasn't interested in attending school dances, parties, or going to "hang out." I was considered a "homebody," because I would rather stay home then go out. My flight pattern started different because I was not your typical teenager. Although, I had friends my age, my preference was to spend time with the elderly.

Life can get in the way of your transition from one stage to the other. Talents we have cannot be utilized if we have the creativity of a butterfly, but we are still wrapped in our cocoon. Remember, "YOLO: You Only Live Once," so we have to embrace each stage in order to appreciate the butterfly effect. I did not value the statement of "you only live once" in the past, but I definitely do now.

There were many things that I did not take advantage of during my cocoon stage. The theory of the butterfly effect is, "when a butterfly moves its wings, it can cause a tornado in another part of the world." The concept sounds unrealistic, but demonstrates that the smallest change can make a big impact in the world. My cocoon stage is an example of how the butterfly effect works. I did not realize the little things I was taught by listening to older women as a teen would cause such a big impact in my life and in the lives of others. I have been able to take the wisdom gained and make an impact in the lives of many women through my experience. I have moved my wings, now I am touching lives of women in different parts of the world as they read this book.

There are women who have made music, voiced their opinions, broken records, suffered ridicule, and changed lives to rise to the top. These women continue to inspire little girls, teens, and women to evolve and discover their dreams. These women were born as an ordinary moth, which evolved into beautiful butterflies. To get where they are, they went through life cycles like all women. Now they are butterflies that have moved their wings in one part of the world causing a major impact that cannot be ignored. Some of these women are: Oprah Winfrey, Hillary Clinton, Mother Teresa, Rosa Parks, Michelle Obama, Beyoncé Knowles, Margaret Thatcher, Lucille Ball, Anne Frank, Toni Morrison, Madame C.J. Walker, Harriet Tubman, Barbara Jordan, there are so many powerful women the list could go on.

You can put the butterfly effect in motion in your life, today. There are small changes you can make now that will make a big impact later. You must focus every day on doing a small task that will allow you to see big changes as time goes on. For instance, if you have a dream or desire to do something, write down the steps it will take to get there and start working on your dream daily.

My hope is for you to recognize what stage of life you are in. It's ok if you remain a cocoon a little longer. Sometimes circumstances keep you in your protective covering a little longer than others. Hopefully as you continue to read, you will find guidance into your metamorphosis and emerge into the beautiful butterfly you were created to be. It's time to love more, laugh more, and learn to live the life you were born to live. Allow your rebirth to start today!

Think About It!
What stage are you in today? What will be your first step in your emergence?

PART

3

The Butterfly

Once a caterpillar transforms into a butterfly, it takes on a whole new shape and form. Initially the wings of the butterfly are pressed against the body, not realizing it has the potential to fly. When it realizes it can fly, the possibilities are endless. Like women, when we see have the capability to find our passion and live out our dreams, we soar.

Butterflies are beautiful free-spirited insects symbolizing freedom and they soar gracefully through the sky. Being empowered and graceful are feelings some women experience and some do not. There are a few women who get to the butterfly stage but never release their wings and realize they have the potential to fly. Other women spread their wings and have the attitude that "the sky is the limit."

Butterfly women soar, exploring possibilities in their relationships, career, birthing books, writing songs, becoming entrepreneurs, and finding their place of happiness in life. Often they release many things they settled for as caterpillars. Once a woman emerges from the caterpillar stage, she evolves into a beautiful butterfly. Women, like butterflies, have their own destiny and no two are alike. Their flight pattern, style, when and where they land, is left up to how far they are willing to spread their wings. You will never fly unless you spread your wings. Are your wings pressed against your body, not allowing you to fly?

Don't wait for opportunities.
 Take simple occasions and
make them great. The weak wait for
opportunities. The strong make them.

CHAPTER

8

Can You Be Lonely, Even Though You Are Not Alone?

"It is strange to be known so universally and yet to be so lonely."

Whether you are single, married, young, or old at some point everyone looks forward to spending time alone. Time alone can be very enjoyable because you are only responsible for entertaining yourself. You may want to sit quietly and read a book, listen to music, or watch a movie. Enjoying your own company is rewarding, it is often much needed and deserved. However, some women feel lonely even when they are with their partners. Loneliness is an empty feeling and can be a feeling of abandonment or rejection. Many women I have talked to are lonely, yet not alone.

There are women who are happy they have found their special someone, whether they are in a committed relationship or married; there are also women who are with someone, but still very lonely. It is difficult emotionally to have a partner, but feel as though you are by yourself. Single women often dream of the day they find that special someone or, "the one" who will be different from the rest. Their hope is that the emptiness they feel will be gone. Countless women change who they are and what they believe in order to capture the attention of a mate thinking they can escape loneliness. Having a mate is more than just having a warm body in the house. If that warm body is there, but there is no connection mentally or emotionally. As my cousin once said,

"Having a mate, who is not emotionally there, is like curtains hanging on the window, they are there, but they aren't fulfilling your emotional needs."

In the beginning of relationships couples feel the need to be together and share every part of them mentally, physically, and emotionally. The desire of togetherness often lasts for months or even a few years. For some couples the time comes when they get settled into a routine and start taking one another's needs for granted. There are changes in relationships that often cause loneliness or distance between couples. The majority of the time, the man doesn't notice there is a problem and feels that everything is "a-ok." Men are more physical and often overlook the emotional side of a relationship as long as their physical needs are met. Some men do not get sensitive, emotional, or even question their spouse or partner if she comes home and doesn't have much to talk about. They may assume, "she must have had a bad day, or it must be her hormones." He will go about his evening without a care in the world. Most of the time, will never question her quietness. Many women on the other hand, will ask a million questions and get frustrated if their mate comes home and doesn't have a lot to say. Most women will question and bother the man so much that before the evening is over, an argument has started. Some arguments can be avoided by giving space and quiet time.

Communication becomes an issue because most men do not feel the need to talk all of the time. Women are emotionally wired, so they feel they need to discuss how they feel and expect the same from the man. Men often feel when they are fulfilling their duties by providing the necessities for the family everything in the home should be good. In a man's eyes everyone should be happy, therefore there's no need for lengthy conversations. It is obvious, from their perspective; they love their family because of what they provide, so they don't feel they should explain anything. The day-to-day functions of work, household responsibilities, children, and other obligations become the basis of the relationship. When there is time for couple's to sit and have alone time, the majority of the time the man will prefer to quietly watch television and the woman will often want to talk. Men may feel that sitting quietly on the couch is spending quality time. Distance grows between the couple, suddenly, the woman feels like she's alone while her partner is sitting right next to her. The man on the other hand, doesn't notice a change in the woman's attitude or demeanor. Oftentimes, men think women just like to nag, are never satisfied, or do not appreciate what he does.

Many women have desires that their partners would express themselves more and want to have the bond they share with their girlfriends; like laughing, gossiping, and just saying whatever is on their mind. When the communication that's expected is not received, women feel distant, rejected, disappointed, and lonely. They start to feel that their dreams, fears, and desires will not be addressed in a meaningful way because they can't talk or express feelings to their partner. There are women who are with their spouse/partners day in and day out and are lonely; they feel their partners take them for granted. There are women who want to be complimented, need affection, and want to feel special, but their men ignore their worth. While she's feeling as though she means nothing to him, he may love her more than words can express, but he doesn't express it, so she doesn't know. Men often brush off lengthy conversations and arguments about what is lacking in the relationship because they don't understand their partner's needs. I have talked to countless women who feel their spouses or partners don't care about them because they don't say how they feel or show physically that their woman is special. The women have said, "I get tons of compliments from other guys, but not from my husband/boyfriend." The feeling explained to me by women, is a feeling of not being appreciated. An older woman once told me, "When partners don't show or tell one another how they feel, it often leads to wondering eyes and accepting attention from someone else."

Many women have said they feel like they have roommates rather than partners. The worse part of loneliness and isolation is when the woman feels like she is not appreciated and feels emotional bondage. If the man does not compliment her, criticizes the way she does things, or makes her feel that she can't make it without him, that is emotional abuse. Worldwide there are women who endure emotional abuse on a day-to-day basis, for years at a time. Men often try to control the relationship and never allow the woman to express her feelings. Usually, if she does express her feelings, the controlling man brushes her off as though what she is saying is irrelevant. Again, that is because the man sees nothing wrong. Women in relationships with controlling men are often lonely and afraid to voice their opinions, which is not healthy. Women remain in relationships captured in a cycle of abuse and loneliness.

The people in the home, the attitudes, and the simple things, can create the environment of a happy home. It doesn't matter how big and beautiful a home is; if there isn't love in the home, there will not be a feeling of warmth and coziness; instead, dread and unhappiness will fill the home. A home with that environment will just be a "house." Some people try to fill the emptiness of their home with "things" to make it feel happy and loving, but there is nothing that money can buy in order to create happiness in an empty relationship.

When we hear the word mansion the first thought comes to mind is a huge house, on acres of land, lavish furniture, many rooms, multiple car garages, and a back yard that has the serenity of the Garden of Eden, landscaped with beautiful flowers, trees, and water fountains. However, a mansion to some can be an apartment with no yard, two bedrooms, and only a carport. Shiny floors, beautiful cabinetry, fancy lighting, and beautifully painted walls, do not make a happy home. A mansion is what you can consider a happy home. The question is…what builds a happy home to turn an ordinary home into a mansion?

There may not be serious issues in the relationship, but if you feel lonely and feel as if there is nothing that can be done to improve the dynamics of the relationship, before you give up, there are things you can try. In order to get attention, you must give attention. Many couples fall into a situation where one will wait for the other to make a move. Couples just settle with the fact that they do not have anything in common, they go their separate ways, live separate lives, sleep in separate rooms, but never try to fix the situation. Relationships in many cases can be reconciled, but it takes patience, willingness, sacrifice, and determination. In today's society, couples want to throw in the towel at the first disagreement rather than tarnish their pride and make a sacrifice. In order for a relationship to succeed, both people must do their part to make it work. One person making changes will not save the relationship. For instance, if your partner isn't talking, start a conversation, if he is sitting on the couch watching television and you want to snuggle, snuggle with him rather than go in another room and think about how lonely you feel and wish he would be more affectionate. If you want to talk, talk to him about things that interest him such as his job, his hobby, or his sport of interest. Give him the same attention that you would want him to give you; you need to be the model of change. Ask him to do the same for you; he may not realize what he is not doing that you want him to do. It is common for women to complain to themselves or their friends about things their partner isn't doing, but they don't talk to their partner. Therefore, quite often the man doesn't know her needs. I've heard women say, "I shouldn't have to tell a grown man how to treat me." While this is true, sometimes you have to be more specific with men. They do not pay attention to emotional details, and they certainly are not mind readers, just as women aren't. Not being sensitive to feelings of one another often leads to distance between the couple, they live together, but are strangers to one another. In most relationships it's a matter of misunderstanding, where the man thinks he's doing all he can, and the woman is feeling like she's doing all she can, but because there is a communication issue, the relationship is in danger.

In addition, to get more out of your relationship with your partner you may need to do things that satisfy yourself without him. This will allow for separate time for each of you to explore interest that you can later come together and talk about. By doing things independently, you will feel empowered and independent which will build your confidence. You won't feel the sting of loneliness all of the time. Many women isolate themselves from friends to fulfill obligations in their relationship. Women should have a social life outside of her relationship to talk to other women and enjoy the laughter and have girl talk. Talk about books you've read, movies you've seen, or fashion trends, do not to sit for hours to gossip about what your mate is or is not doing. It's okay if your friend is someone you can trust, but it is rare to find someone who will listen to your relationship issues and not feel compelled to share it with someone else. Women often find out that their friends are experiencing the same aloneness. Finding someone who can relate to you is often a relief and helps you not feel like you are in a hopeless situation, but again, don't let dome and gloom or a relationship be the topic of your girl time together. The purpose of girl time is to clear your mind to refocus. If being with other women or having girl time isn't something you want to do, make a list of things you can do alone like sewing, reading, gardening, listening to music, or watching a chick flick. As women we all have our own personality, some women want to socialize, while others do not. Learning to be happy alone is a great accomplishment to avoid loneliness in a relationship.

Women who are in the caterpillar stage have a very difficult time with loneliness because they are vulnerable and needy, whereas a woman who has emerged into the butterfly stage will do various things to get her partners attention, if he does not respond, she learns to embrace her alone time. This is usually the time the butterfly finds her passion and discovers her dream because she focuses her energy on things that make her happy and does not depend solely on her relationship to fulfill her happiness.

Think About It!
If you are in a lonely relationship, what are you going to do to change it?

Emotions don't make noise.
You can't hear pride, caring is
faint. Love is so quiet sometimes you
don't know it's there.

CHAPTER

9

How to Walk, Talk, and Act like A Lady
Being a Female Does Not Automatically Make You Lady.

It's very important for females to know the difference between a lady and a woman. Throughout this book topics regarding women's issues have been discussed, however it's important for females to know simple things such as how to present yourself as a lady. It's like knowing the difference between a caterpillar and a butterfly. Ladies are not born, they are made. The quicker women understand, just because you are a female does not automatically make you a lady, the easier it will be to adapt to the role of a lady; the type that can go anywhere at any time with anyone. Be the type of lady who could go as a guest at the Whitehouse, attend a red carpet event, the Oscars, or just hanging out with your girlfriends sitting around the kitchen table drinking tea. Ladies will be a lady wherever they go. In order to perfect the role of a lady you must learn through observing, reading, understanding, and practicing. Initially, women feel unnatural when they try to adapt to the ladylike behavior, because they feel they act too formal all of the time. You have to find a new balance in the way you carry yourself, anything new feels different. Celebrating your femininity means being a lady.

In the past we have all heard, "ladies should be seen, not heard." Women in the past were in the background, taking care of families, working inside of the home, not having much say so regarding decisions in the home, politics, or otherwise, they were to be quiet. Ladies of the past dressed a certain way; they could not bring attention to themselves by wearing clothes that showed their skin, or makeup to adorn their beauty, their hair was usually pulled back in a tight bun. As young girls growing up, we were taught certain rules or manners that our mothers passed down from their mothers or grandmother's, but it was more less, manners, not etiquette. For instance, red nail polish or lipstick was a forbidden color for women because the color red was associated with "ladies of the night."

There is a difference between manners and etiquette. Manners say a lot about us, they tell how you were brought up, what kind of person you are, the extent of your reading and traveling experiences. People with good manners can lack education, wealth, etc. and people will overlook it if manners are intact. Manners are kind, considerate, things that are done to consider the thoughts and feelings of others. You may say what's the difference between manners and etiquette? Etiquette can be compared to laws or rules, for those of you who have read books on etiquette; you will see a list of rules. Such as how to properly set the table, what utensils should be used when eating certain foods, when to speak, and what to say are all rules of etiquette. While manners are taught, etiquette is acquired over time.

Being a lady has different meanings for different people, part of being a lady means being graceful. Social grace ensures that you will likely be invited to popular parties, be the respected well-liked girl in the office, it can even help you capture the man of your dreams.

There are quick tips that ladies can use to navigate in today's society. It's important to present the best version of you especially if you are in search of your Mr. Right. Being a lady is a full-time job; you should always be generous and present a humble character.

Here are a few perils of wisdom that ladies need to keep in the forefront of their minds on how to be a lady:

- A lady never rushes-she is conscious of time and doesn't commit to so many obligations that she always arrives to her destination out of breath, with her head down to avoid embarrassment, or is known by everyone for being late.

- Ladies are gentle, not rude, or moody, but they have a consistent character. You treat everyone with the same respect and choose your friends wisely.

- Ladies use tactful speech; never use inappropriate words, especially, not in front of strangers. Always be mindful of what you say and how you say it.

- Ladies are always appropriately dressed and makes every effort to keep her appearance together. Even a quick run to the grocery store, a lady should make sure she is presentable, it shows that she took time and pride in her appearance before leaving home.

- Ladies should be beautiful inside and out. If you are gorgeous on the outside, but your insides are full of resentment, hatefulness, and does not forgive easily, it takes away from your beauty.

- Ladies should be kind, but not a doormat. You should defend yourself if you are in a situation that you need to, but always maintain composure and self-control.

- Ladies are responsible, trustworthy, and never drinks in excess.

Character of a Lady

- Remain composed in all situations and remains calm, never yelling or screaming in or out of public. Remember, "Ladies should be seen, not heard."

• Give praise to others, ladies do not try to keep attention on them, if it should be on someone else.

• Do not have an, I- know -it-all attitude, even if you are well educated, you will always remain humble and will never make someone feel beneath you.

• Never brag or make light of your accomplishment when you are praised.

Quality is a must to elegance. Ladies should aim for quality over quantity. Good quality lasts for a long time. Life in today's society may be changing, but the qualities of a true lady are timeless. True ladies possess a combination of grace, charm, and elegance.

In order for a lady to emerge and evolve into a butterfly, she must know how to conduct herself to soar in society.

Think About It!
Do you present yourself as a female, or a lady?

At some point in your life you will realize who really matters, who never did, and who always will.

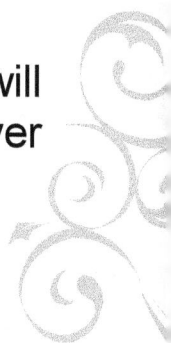

CHAPTER

10

Older, Wiser, Better

"The first half of a woman's life belongs to everyone else, the second half should belong to her."- Pitre-Frazier

Becoming a butterfly is a beautiful, yet challenging transformation. Once the transformation is complete the freedom felt inside is like no other. Many women struggle through each stage, but once they evolve there is a feeling of wholeness and unstoppable independence. It is an awkward feeling emerging from a caterpillar, evolving to a butterfly. As the transformation is taking place women experience changes in the way they think, how they feel, what they will tolerate, and often experience changes in relationships. Relationships with spouses, boyfriends, family members, and anyone else who is a part of the woman's life, often feel the transformation. A transforming caterpillar does not have the tolerance for foolishness. Many women find they feel things that were once important are now irrelevant. For instance, there have been long friendships/relationships that have ended because a woman coming into her own feels that trivial things and people need to be moved out of her life. There is a level of tolerance when women get to certain stage in their lives that they appear to others to be irritable, actually it's that the person has crossed the, what I call, the *"no foolery line."* Some women play hide and seek behind their Superwoman mask and cape for years, hiding their emotions, and fears. Their face shows strength, happiness, and peace, while their insides are weak, sad, and crumbling. Being able to evolve takes courage, it seems to some that they are stuck, and will never escape their cocoon, however it can be done.

There are times women need to:

- Stop analyzing the past

- Stop planning the future

- Stop trying to figure out how we feel

- Stop deciding with our mind what we want our heart to feel.

Sometimes we must go with the feelings we have, whatever happens…happens. As women prepare their journey to soar as a butterfly, they must understand that the journey will not be easy and the decisions she makes should be her own. People will always have advice, but the ultimate decision has to be your decision, because at the end of the day, when you lay your head on your pillow you must be able to close your eyes in peace and get a good night's sleep knowing you have made decisions from your heart.

Many women in the butterfly stage have tough decisions to make, "Should I stay on this dead end job, Should I continue to be unhappy in this loveless relationship, Should I continue to put everyone else's feelings in front of mine?" These are all life changing decisions, therefore, a woman in the butterfly stage must not make decisions in a hurry, but have all of the details planned and ready to execute. As some women get older it appears they get braver and are ready to take the world head on. It is often said there is a mindset shift in women between the ages of 40 and 50, things that were important are no longer priority anymore, time is of essence and happiness seems to climb to #1 on their list of what they need. There are countless women who feel they have given the best they had to offer as a wife, mother, employee, friend, and other roles they have played in everyone else's life. It is now their time to live and enjoy the second half of their life.

I have had the pleasure to be blessed with phenomenal examples of butterflies in my life. However, it wasn't until I realized the cycles of transformation that I was able to say, "Hey, I've met some true butterflies!" Age brings about appreciation for different experiences in life. When you are young you don't realize lessons being taught, or people being placed in your life for distinct purposes. All of which will later come together like a puzzle. I felt equipped for the role of mother and wife due to the examples of my true butterflies.

Although my mother can be described as a loner, she lived her life as an example of always providing her services to others. She never talked on the phone a lot or visited much, but if anyone needed her she was always there to help. Growing up, she was the neighbor and friend who would be Florence Nightingale to everyone. She would go to the store for those who were unable to go for themselves, sit with the sick, give clothes to the needy, and always looked for ways to help others. Besides my mother, I was blessed to have two grandmothers and a great grandmother. All three of them played different roles in my life, yet were very much a part of me becoming the woman I am today. On my mother's side I had a grandmother and great grandmother who were both very quiet women. I would always enjoy going to their home because of the peace and quiet that was felt, there was never chaos, or people coming in and out of their home. I observed them in their roles as one cooked, the other cleaned, they were true examples of teamwork. My grandmother taught me how to bake cakes, and I looked forward to that on Saturday evenings. We would bake a cake on Saturday evening for dessert on Sunday. My great grandmother was the best "ironer" (yes I made that word up), I had ever seen. She would iron everything in the house, pillowcases, sheets, dishcloths, you name it. If it could have a wrinkle she would iron it! I have pleasant, calming memories of the weekends I would spend with them. They taught me to be content without a lot of busy bodies in my home and that there were always chores to do, you should never be bored.

Then there was my dad's mother, "Big Mama," she was an angel and a butterfly. As a child I attended church, but never really understood what was being taught. I learned more from Big Mama about the Bible and how to live a Christian life sitting on her front porch then I did going to church on Sunday's. She was truly a God-fearing and spiritual woman, who truly led by example. I spent a lot of time under her wings, sitting on her porch. We lived across the street from her, so I would visit her every day. When I was in elementary school, my sisters and I would stay with Big Mama until my mother got home from work. I will always remember our snack of toast with peach jelly; she made the best toast ever! She was known by all of her grandchildren for her stew, okra, and hot cornbread. That was her signature meal no one ever got tired of eating it.

Another memory of Big Mama was the way she chastised us. When we would do something wrong, she would make us recite a Bible verse related to what we did wrong, or she would get a brown paper bag and a pencil, we would have to write a Bible verse. For instance, if we were upset because our parents told us to do something, she would talk to us, say a prayer, afterwards we would have to write Ephesians 6: 1-3. If we argued, told a falsehood, or had an attitude, there would be a scripture for us to learn. She was always positive, if anyone would go to her upset or complaining about something or someone, her advice was always, to pray about it. Big Mama was indeed a true prayer warrior. As long as I can remember, she prayed faithfully when she woke up, 9:00 am, 12:00 noon, 3:00 pm, 6:00 pm, and before she went to bed. Up until her death she lived her life as a true example of a Christian. Lessons of life she taught me were always appreciated, but as I grew older, I began to realize just how valuable they were. I often reflect on things

Big Mama taught. I remember like yesterday, the times we would sit on her porch and talk, never realizing at the time that I was a butterfly in training. Once I became a married woman and mother I often said, "Big Mama had some big shoes to fill." Living the life she lived wasn't easy, but she made it look like it was.

I was fortunate as a young, new, wife to have neighbors who were always there for me when I needed them. My husband worked a lot; therefore, I was home alone quite often. Initially, when I would be home at night, I would be afraid. We lived on a dark street, plus, I wasn't used to being home alone for long periods of time in a new place. My fear quickly went away when I met my new neighbors. Mr. and Mrs. Provost lived next door to us; they were in their 70s when I met them. I remember talking to Mrs. Provost for the first time, she comforted me and assured me if I needed them any time of the day or night, they would come over if I called. They had a farm with cows, horses, pigs, chickens, and dogs. Mr. Provost was a very quiet man, but he was a very hard worker. I would always look out of the window and see him tending to his animals early in the morning, or sitting under his carport in the late afternoon after a hard day's work. Now, Mrs. Provost truly earned her secret nickname I gave her, I called, "my real life May West." She would work on the farm as hard as her husband. She would drive the tractor, milk the cows, feed the chickens, and walk through the pigpens with her knee length rubber boots; then go in and cook a hot meal. Her house was always immaculate.

One funny memory was that she always had her keys hooked on the belt loops of her pants. I think she had 100 keys on that key ring! I always thought to myself, she must have the keys to the city! The first time I saw her in action outside on the farm, I was like, "Whoa, how can she do that in the hot sun? Ugh, that's gross!" Once I became acquainted with her, I enjoyed going to her house, sitting down talking to her and her husband. She never complained, she was a strong woman who feared nothing, she exemplified fearlessness. I witnessed and learned the meaning of a fearless woman from her.

We have all heard stories about evil, nosey, protective mother-in-laws. I was blessed to have the greatest mother-in-law ever! The first time I met her, of course, I was afraid because she appeared to be a serious woman. I wasn't sure if that was her personality or if she didn't like me. After being around her a few more times, I realized she was a very sweet but stern woman. She had to be a strong disciplinarian because when her husband passed away she still had children to rear as a single parent. It was obvious by her demeanor that she was no-nonsense. However, we got along great! She exemplified the spirit of an obedient woman of Christ. Her knowledge of the Bible and her character radiated spiritual light. She had skills in the kitchen that could not be beat. Prior to meeting her, I had never tasted biscuits, cakes, pies, or tea cakes (all from scratch) as delicious as hers. I spent time with her, and often called her for guidance trying to learn her skills in the kitchen. I would watch her bake, and cook, but quickly learned to just eat and enjoy because she didn't measure anything, so it was difficult, if not impossible to duplicate her dishes. She was indeed a phenomenal woman, not only was she a great cook and baker, her ability to sew and crochet were untouchable! The word "mother-in-law," had a different meaning for me, it meant "phenomenal woman."

People come into our lives for reasons and seasons. Some people come in our lives to stay, some as a blessing, some as a lesson, and some we never really know why they came. We all have butterflies that have taught us the basics of soaring, but we must use the examples to grow. We can't put the examples on a shelf in our memory bank. Life experiences are not always comfortable; sometimes we have to experience discomfort in order to get to comfortable. We all experience things in life that may not feel so good, but there is a reason for the discomfort. Discomfort often comes about when you are experiencing a transformation. We don't always take advantage of our lessons, we complain, mope, or get discouraged. Some people embrace life lessons, and some will reject them. Attitude has a lot to do with whether or not your life lessons are difficult or easy. As a woman in the butterfly stage you may learn the importance of the Law of Attraction and having a positive attitude. The Law of Attraction is belief that "like attracts like," it teaches that every positive or negative event that happens to you is attracted by you.

I started visualizing what I wanted to attract, how I wanted my life to be, and how I wanted my life story to change. My transformation began four months before my 50th birthday, which I can remember as if it were yesterday. I continued to wrestle with the feeling of wanting to do more than I was doing in my relationship, career, and my life overall. I felt something was changing within. I wasn't afraid; it was a good feeling, a sense of peace and freedom. I remember feeling something inside trying to get out of my body for a few years. As mentioned in an earlier chapter, many women experience the feeling that they cannot be who they really are because of various reasons. For years I felt this strong woman within me, but it wasn't her season to come out. God was preparing her to make her debut. I remember saying to myself, I want to do more then be a wife, mother, or employee. I have been someone to everyone else, but myself. It is now time for me! It was at that moment I began to be more vocal in my relationship with my husband, friends, family, and anyone else in my life. It was at that point that I realized that I am a grown woman," I have a voice, I have a life, and I'm living it!"

The first thing I did was I learned the power, value and liberation of the word, "NO." I was able to say "no" without conviction or guilt. There have been many times in my life that I would do things that I really didn't want to do in order to make someone else happy, not realizing that I was the one who suffered in the end. You will know in your heart when it's ok to say "no." You have to get to the point where saying "no" won't make you feel bad. Once you say "no" to something you really don't want to do, or don't agree with without guilt, you have learned the art "no." Think of the many times you have done something, gone someplace, or committed to something you never wanted to do in the beginning, yet you did it because, you didn't want to let someone else down, but while they are excited and happy you are feeling like, "I should not have committed to this, I don't want to be here, or do this." Ultimately, the person that suffers from saying yes when they wanted to say no is you. The first few times you practice saying no, it will feel awkward, but once you get comfortable, you will sit back, say no, cross your legs, pour a glass of tea, open your favorite book, and never look back. It is such a liberating feeling to say no and begin to live your life on your own terms!

Not all women actually feel when they evolve into their butterfly stage as I did. In order to become a butterfly, you have to appreciate the journey. Once I experienced my freedom to be me and found my life's purpose, I took a deep breath, looked up and thanked God. I felt so light on the inside, no longer feeling the need to carry the burden of the inner me being suppressed. In order to feel the evolvement you must pay attention and listen to the calm, still voice. By spending time alone and getting to know yourself, you give yourself permission to spread your wings and soar. Don't be afraid to evolve, each of us has a life of purpose and if we don't discover our purpose we live a life of emptiness and not being fulfilled. As we get older, we should get wiser and reflect on lessons we have learned. Don't simply live life, learn to love life.

Think About It!
Can you say no and feel good about it? Are you just living
life, or do you love life?

Winners make goals, losers
make excuses. Excuses won't bring
Dreams 2 Reality.

MESSAGE FROM THE AUTHOR

"Women in particular need to keep an eye on their physical and mental health, because if we're scurrying to and from appointments and errands, we don't have a lot of time to take care of ourselves. We need to do a better job of putting ourselves higher on our own 'to do' list."
– Michelle Obama

The quote by Michelle Obama sums up my inspiration for writing this book. *The Butterfly Effect: Transform From Your Cocoon* is a book intended to nurture, connect, share wisdom, and motivate women to emerge in order to discover who they are and become all they dream of. Women often give up who they are to fulfill roles in the lives of others. As Mrs. Obama said, as women we must put "ourselves higher on our own 'to do' list." Throughout this book, I shared obstacles I have faced in my life trying to juggle being "Superwoman." My journey from my cocoon to where I am as a butterfly wasn't always an easy road. There is no doubt God had my hand in His hand throughout my journey. There were times I would have given up if I had relied on my own strength. I spent lots of hours praying and fasting to make it from one stage in life to the next. Each obstacle was a stepping stone to the freedom I have in my life now. I made many sacrifices to be the best me that I knew how to be. As I reflect on my life, I never had this chapter written in my life's story; that I would be an entrepreneur, or an author. That's how I know we do not have the transcript of how the story of our lives will end.

For a very long time, I did not have any goals or plans outside of being an educator until retirement. I knew I had more to offer women, but did not have an idea of how I would reach masses of women. I never knew I would be speaking to audiences; again God had a bigger plan for me. Had it not been for God's grace and mercy, had He not orchestrated the unfortunate situation that occurred at my former place of employment, I would not have pursued my dreams and passions. At the time I did not know why it happened, but as I look back, I am so thankful! I praise God and give Him the glory. He was directing my steps and protecting me all along. He knew when my time was up at that job. He knew how my next chapter of life would be. His timing is always perfect. All we have to do in life is be obedient and not give up when the going gets tough.

My hope is that you spend quality time reading this book to absorb the information to enhance your growth and development. As you read each chapter, read with an open mind and a heart willing to give you the courage to think outside the box. I believe every individual deserves more than one chance in life to be happy. We are all on a spiritual journey to create our own reality. God gave all of us permission to be happy.

I have been blessed with the gift to help people get to a place of self-knowledge and to experience their personal and professional fulfillment. Because of my personal life experiences, I understand isolation and aloneness. Although at some point in life everyone experiences pain, but pain doesn't last forever unless you allow it to. My passion is to develop dreams; I value freedom. We all have the ability to be set free and to become new from the inside out. All butterflies begin as a cocoon; they emerge beautifully and are set free, symbolizing freedom. Everyone has their own journey to do what creates happiness and fulfillment in their lives.

Just as I decided to follow my dreams and passions when I was given a chance, you too can follow yours. Today is the beginning of the rest of your life, be excited to see where your dreams take you. Now it is time for you to go into the world, spread your wings and fly! There will not be a conclusion to this book because I do not know where God is going to take me next. ☺

Be Blessed,

Darolyn
Dreams2RealityCoach

Be thankful for your life no matter what you are going through. Somebody, somewhere would trade their life for yours.

Testimonials

"Darolyn brings from the heart to this book what she not only knows, but she has lived. Some of it I have witnessed for years and can say the only change I've seen is a "wiser, more confident, vibrant woman." A woman who is willing to share her life and lifestyle to help any and all who needs it or wants it. As you read and embrace the wisdom shared on each page you'll easily relate to the truth and be ready and willing to be transformed into the butterfly you are intended to be. I love you Darolyn and I'm proud of you." ~ Your Sister, Joe Ann

Darolyn is an outstanding life coach and confidante that listens and gives you the honest truth. She has been a very instrumental influence in my life and I know you all will love her just as much as I do. ~ S. Searles

I met Darolyn at a vulnerable stage in my life. I was a sixteen year old who desperately fought to find herself while dealing with an alcoholic father and an unstable long distant relationship.

Those near and dear to me described me as a closed book, hopeless, a statistic waiting to happen but Darolyn didn't judge this book by the cover. Instead, she listened, dug deep and helped a flower bloom. She listened without trying to mold me or change my wants and needs. She did not overpower me with her opinions; she helped me develop my own solutions while also empowering me and providing a powerhouse of support.

Twenty five years later, I can say with confidence, Darolyn has been the constant thread of stability and balance in my life. As I overcome obstacles and continue my journey, I often reflect on Darolyn's sound advice to keep my health and happiness first. It works; try it!

Thank you Lord for sending Darolyn to rescue and aid me during some of my most trying moments. ~ YOLO (you only live once)

Where do I start? I'm sure it'll be edited but it's from my heart. I didn't have a relationship with you growing up and often envied my other cousins that were in your wedding your children always received the nice compliments from family members and it seemed like I always tried to fit in. I do remember our relationship changing for the better after I started college we'd talk daily (always on the weekends) and you never seemed too busy. As time progressed, I learned more about relationships and as we'd talked more, I learned more but still not applying it. Every time I met a guy "he'd be the one" and when I became nervous "my stomach would hurt." Never did you judge me and always listened when I talked, cried, babbled, etc. After I had AJ, met my hubby, had Eric, my granny/mama passed, my mom was extremely ill, the issues with my dad and we finished our master degrees, our relationship continued to blossom to immeasurable levels!

"If you can believe it, you can achieve it!" I thank God for you and our relationship daily. Proverbs 27:17 NLT 'As iron sharpens iron, so a friend sharpens a friend.' Thanks for being you, genuine, empathetic, and unconditional love all qualities of a great counselor, mentor, mother, aunt, sister, friend, a virtuous woman congrats auntie your favorite niece ME! ~ Shari

So much to share about a phenomenal woman...Darolyn inspires me and my family with love and friendship. My teenage daughter had some past issues bottled up. Darolyn counseled her with patience and loyalty. Her determination and passion inspired my daughter to be respectfully open. I believe it takes a village to raise children. I am blessed to have known and love a wonderful woman like Darolyn. May God continue to bless " My DeeDee" on her journey... ~Brandy Thorne AKA "Aunt B"

Darolyn has a passion for helping others truly transform their lives by helping them understand the power of communication and the importance of building strong healthy relationships. Her own powerful personal story of transformation makes her easy to relate to and a joy to work with. I am truly blessed to have had the opportunity to watch her grow and spread her wings. I wish her much VIP Success in every endeavor. ~Monique Spence, VIP Performance Coach

This testimony, to some, may seem biased being that Darolyn is my mother. Honestly, the words that I type come from the heart of a growing woman, not someone who wants to put her mother on a pedestal. That being said, my mother has been a friend, confidant, and role model to virtually everyone she has met. When I was younger, I remember having company and we would follow her from room to room laughing, talking, and telling her all of our secrets. She has always been the type of person who calmly listened to the situations of others and gave her advice only when she was asked. I've always felt blessed to have a mother who allowed my sister and me to come to her with ANYTHING and if she didn't know the answers (which most of the time she did) *insert smile* she would help us iron out the kinks until we felt better. My mom taught me to have a positive outlook on life and I follow that advice to the fullest. My glass is always half full not half empty. I love you, Mama and I'm happy to see you doing what you have always done so naturally! Rise to the top!!!! ~ Richelle

I know Tupac already came up with this song but he didn't write about my mama so I won't make this long. Thank you for being my inspiration because since I was a girl you told me I could be anything I wanted across the nation. There aren't enough words in the dictionary to describe a woman like you and every single day I see you working hard to make your dreams come true. I watched you from a caterpillar and then you morphed into a butterfly and now that your book is launching I want you to fly high! Thank you for being the best mother in the world and I want to say I love you from your baby girl! ~ Richae'

Over the course of a 20+ yr friendship, I've never known anyone more humble to mankind who's always willing to help others in any form or fashion. A confidant who never meets a stranger, great at listening and slow to speak when giving great advice. One of the greatest human beings I know: admiral dtr/wife/mom/grandmother/teacher, and lastly but not least, an awesome friend and sister in The WORD who mostly leads by example. I love her like the sister I never had...there's not much she doesn't know SOMETHING ABOUT and always willing to seek out if she doesn't. Always growing never stagnant. She's helped me and numerous others in various facets of our lives. Let her help you in yours... I was listening to the View this says it best... 'you have WALKING UNCONDITIONAL LOVE for human kind...' a great mentor ~ Cheryl R.

Think About It! Book Club Questions

- What treasures are inside of your box waiting for permission to come out?

- Are you getting a new life, or settling for the life you are living?

- What is the face saying that's looking at you when you look in the mirror?

- Have you had to re-route your GPS to guide you in the right direction?

- Are you being yourself or wishing you could trade places and be someone else?

- Do you have what it takes to be a confident woman?

- What stage are you in today? What will be your first step in your emergence?

- If you are in a lonely relationship, what are you going to do to change it?

- Do you present yourself as a female, or a lady?

- Can you say no and feel good about it? Are you just living life, or do you love life?

www.ingramcontent.com/pod-product-compliance
Lightning Source LLC
Chambersburg PA
CBHW060413090426
42734CB00011B/2303